© Bob Clemenz

1

© Bruce Finchum

Mexican Gold Poppy

The Mexican Gold poppy (Eschscholtzia mexicana) carpets the desert floor with its magnificent hues of orange and yellow during the spring months of February through May. A close relative of the California Poppy, this four-petal flower is found blooming across the desert and lining the desert highways after heavy summer rains.

© Bruce Finchum

© Bruce Finchum

3

Brittlebush with Lupine and Indian Paintbrush.
© Bruce Finchum

© Bruce Finchum

Brittlebush

The Brittlebush (Encelia farinosa) is a great example of how plants have adapted to the desert. The brittlebush, named after its very brittle stems, actually has two sets of leaves that grow depending on current climate conditions. When the climate is cooler and has more moisture pale green leaves appear. These leaves are designed to absorb a lot of sunlight. During the intense summer heat another set of leaves grow. These leaves have a layer of white hairs that acts as a sun block to protect the leaves from getting burned. During the spring, brittlebush dramatically paints the rocky hillsides and flats with its dazzling yellow color.

Brittlebush with Chuparosa
© Terry Donnelly

5

Pincushion cactus
(Mammillaria microcarpa)
© Richard Reynolds

Golden Cascade (Coryphanta recuvata)
© Bruce Griffin

Rainbow Cactus (Echinocereus pectinatus)
© Steve Rasmussen

Rainbow Cactus (Echinocereus dasyacanthus)
© Laurence Parent

© Neil Weidner

Bladderpod (Lesquerella Gordoni)
© Dietrich Photography

Desert Mariposa (Calochortus kennedyi)
© Bruce Griffin

Barrel Cactus

The Barrel Cactus (Ferocactus wislizenii) is unlike most other cacti in the southwest desert because it blooms in the late summer as opposed to the spring. The blossoms vary in color from yellow, orange, and red and are found growing in a ring at the top of the cactus.

Barrell © Bruce Finchum

© Bruce Finchum

© Smith-Southwestern, Inc.

© Bruce Finchum

Prickly Pear

The Prickly Pear Cactus (Opuntia paecantha) is a reliable source of beauty every spring. Even after a year with little winter rain, the yellow and reddish flowers on this remarkable species will still bloom. In addition to the cactus being attractive, the prickly pear fruit is also a source of food for animals and people. The fruit is used throughout the southwest to make jellies, fruits and other various foods.

© Bruce Finchum   © Ryan Finchum

Sand Verbena (Abronia villosa) © Terry Donnelly

Claret Cup (Echinocereus triglochidiatus) © Gary Rassmussen

Texas Bluebonnets (Lupinus sp.) © Richard Reynolds

Owl's Clover (Orthocarpus purpuranscens) © Bob Clemenz

13

© Bruce Finchum

Ocotillo

Ocotillo (Fouquieria splendens) is an enchanting plant found in the southwest desert. It has long stems that grow up to 30 feet tall. These thorny stems are typically leafless, but when the soil is moist after the winter rain they develop bright green leaves. Between March and May, the Ocotillo stems bloom with red tubular flowers.

© Bruce Finchum

© Bruce Finchum

Beavertail cactus (*Opuntia basilaris*)
© Edgar Callaert

© Bruce Griffin

Indian Paintbrush (Castilleja angustifolia)
© Terry Donnelly

Globe Mallow (Sphaeralcea ambigua) © Neil Weidner

© Bruce Finchum

(Coryphantha sp.)
© Peter Noebels

© Richard Reynolds

20

Desert Star (Monoptilon bellioides) © Steve Rasmussen

Fishhook Cactus (Mammilaria grahamii) © Steve Rasmussen

21

Cholla Cactus

Many varieties of the Cholla cactus (Opuntia sp.) can be seen when traveling through the desert. Cholla cacti are made up of joints that can detach easily. Its spines can lock onto objects that closely pass by. (Sometimes referred to as the "jumping cactus" because it seems as though the cactus joint must have jumped off the plant onto the nearest object.) Having this ability makes it easier for the cactus to spread. The sections that detach can fall onto the ground and grow a new plant.

© Bruce Finchum

© Fawn Finchum

Hedgehog cactus

Hedgehog cacti (Echinocereus engelmannii) have stylish blooms in a variety of colors from purple to magenta. The spines grow up to 4 inches long in order to protect the blooms. The hedgehog cactus has adapted to the harsh conditions of the desert by evolving into a plant with a shallow root system that allow the cactus to grow where little water is available.

23

Dune Evening Primrose (Oenothera deltoides)
© Mary Liz Austin

Nodding thistle (Cirisum sp.)
© Neil Weidner

Long leaf morning glory
© Bruce Griffen

**Arizona Blue Eyes
(Evolvulus arizonicus)**
© Bruce Griffen

© Bruce Finchum

Thorn-Apple (Datura wrightii)
© Bruce Griffin

*"Devil's Claw" or Unicorn Plant
(Proboscidea altheaefolia)*
© Bruce Griffin

**Queen-of-the-night cactus
(Peniovereus greggii)**
© Neil Weidner

**Prickly poppy
(Argemone
pleiacantha)**
© Neil Weidner

25

Paloverde Tree
(Cercidium floridum)

Century plants

Century plants (Agave deser-ti), also called desert agave, can grow up to 40 feet tall. They bloom only once in the plants lifetime when it is be-tween 10 and 20 years old and usually during the month of June. The tall stalk may re-main for a short time after, but the plant dies once it has bloomed. The Indians once used the stiff leaves as a source of nutrition.

© Terry Donnelly

© Bruce Griffin

Joshua Tree

The Joshua Tree (Yucca brevifolia) fruit blooms between March and May and relies on a female moth to spread the pollen which enables the plant to reproduce. These mysterious plants can grow to a height of 15 to 40 feet tall and the arms can be one to three feet wide.

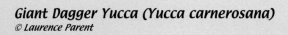

Giant Dagger Yucca (Yucca carnerosana)
© Laurence Parent

Yucca (Yucca elata)
© *Bruce Finchum*

© Bruce Finchum

30

© Bruce Finchum

Saguaro

The Saguaro Cactus (Carnegia gigantea) is the most notable icon for southwest desert. This gigantic cactus can reach heights of 50 feet and weights of 9 tons. Some of have been found to be living for more than 200 years. Many desert animals, such as the elf owls and cactus wrens, make their homes in this large cactus. The white flowers of the Saguaro bloom during the month of May and can be seen from a great distance as they often tower above the other desert vegetation.

© Laurence Parent